D1451473

ARMED FORCES

★ ★ ★

UNITED STATES

AIR FORCE

by Derek Zobel

Falcon Elementary
School Library

™

This edition first published in 2008 by Bellwether Media.

No part of this publication may be reproduced in whole
or in part without written permission of the publisher.
For information regarding permission, write to Bellwether
Media Inc., Attention: Permissions Department,
Post Office Box 19349, Minneapolis, MN 55419-0349.

Library of Congress
Zobel, Derek, 1983–
  United States Air Force / by Derek Zobel.
    p. cm. — (Torque: Armed Forces)
  Includes bibliographical references and index.
  ISBN-13: 978-1-60014-161-4 (hbk. : alk. paper)
  ISBN-10: 1-60014-161-7 (hbk. : alk. paper)
  1. United States. Air Force—Juvenile literature. I. Title.
  UG633.Z63 2008
  358.400973–dc22   2007042406

CONTENTS

★ ★ ★

★ ★ ★

Chapter One

WHAT IS THE UNITED STATES AIR FORCE?

The United States Air Force patrols the skies and protects the country from threats. It also transports military equipment and supports civilian aircraft during emergencies.

The United States Air Force is one of five branches of the **United States Armed Forces**. The other four branches are the Army, Coast Guard, Marine Corps, and Navy. The five branches work together to defend the nation. The Air Force used to be a part of the United States Army. It became its own branch of the Armed Forces in 1947.

Chapter Two

VEHICLES, WEAPONS, AND TOOLS OF THE AIR FORCE

When two fighter planes are engaged in combat, it is called a dogfight.

The U.S. Air Force uses a wide variety of aircraft to accomplish **missions**. Bombers attack enemy bases and military factories from high in the sky. Fighter planes protect other planes. They fire **machine guns** and launch **missiles** at enemy aircraft. They can also carry bombs and launch attacks. The most well-known fighter plane of the U.S. Air Force is the F-16 Fighting Falcon.

The F-16 Fighting Falcon can go faster than 1,500 miles (2,400 kilometers) per hour.

F-22 Raptor

B-2 Spirit

Radar

All aircraft are equipped with basic technology such as **radar**. Radar uses radio waves to find objects in the air. Pilots and air force bases can detect enemy planes. Some aircraft have newer technology. The F-22 Raptor and the B-2 Spirit have **stealth** technology. It allows them to hide from enemy radar.

A B-2 stealth bomber costs more than $2 billion to build.

The nose of a
C-5 Galaxy opens
to load cargo.

AIR NAT[...]

The Air Force also uses huge transport planes to move vehicles and equipment. The C-130 Hercules and the C-5 Galaxy transport troops, vehicles, and equipment all over the world. They are two of the largest aircraft ever built. The C-5 Galaxy has a wingspan of 222.9 feet (67.9 meters). It can carry 270,000 pounds (122,472 kilograms) of cargo.

ONAL GUARD

C-5 Galaxy

A pilot and two sensor operators control drones from the ground.

14

Drone

Unmanned **drones** are new tools for the Air Force. Drones are able to fight the enemy from the air without risking a pilot's life. Drones were first designed for **reconnaissance**. They have since been armed with missiles and bombs.

Chapter Three

LIFE IN THE AIR FORCE

The Air Force provides many different opportunities for airmen and airwomen. They can serve as pilots, technicians, mechanics, or healthcare personnel. All members of the Air Force serve on an Air Force base. Air Force bases offer living quarters, schools, hospitals, parks, and more.

Most men and women in the Air Force are **enlisted members**. They begin their service in **basic training**. They take classes and do exercises. More specific training follows basic training. Some airmen and airwomen become mechanics and work on aircraft. Others learn about electronics and become technicians.

Mechanic

Only officers can become pilots.

Officers are in charge of the enlisted members. They must have a college degree. Many attend the Air Force Academy in Colorado. Officers get even more training at the Air Force's Officer Candidate School (OCS). They learn about leadership and how to carry out missions. They make the decisions and provide the leadership to help keep the United States safe.

GLOSSARY

★ ★ ★

basic training—the course of drills, tests, and military training that new enlisted members of every branch of the U.S. Armed Forces must go through

drone—a type of unmanned, remote-controlled aircraft

enlisted member—a person in the U.S. Armed Forces who ranks below an officer; all enlisted members are currently volunteers.

machine gun—an automatic weapon that rapidly fires bullets

missile—an explosive launched at targets on the ground or in the air

mission—a military task

officer—a member of the armed forces who has a rank above enlisted members

radar—a sensor system that uses radio waves to locate objects in the air

reconnaissance—secret observation

stealth—designed to avoid detection

United States Armed Forces—the five branches of the United States military; they are the Air Force, the Army, the Coast Guard, the Marine Corps, and the Navy.

TO LEARN MORE

★ ★ ★

AT THE LIBRARY

David, Jack. *B-2 Stealth Bombers*. Minneapolis, Minn.: Bellwether, 2008.

David, Jack. *F-16 Fighting Falcons*. Minneapolis, Minn.: Bellwether, 2008.

Donovan, Sandra. *The U.S. Air Force*. Minneapolis, Minn.: Lerner, 2004.

Hopkins, Ellen. *The United States Air Force*. Chicago, Ill.: Heinemann, 2002.

ON THE WEB

Learning more about the United States Air Force is as easy as 1, 2, 3.

1. Go to www.factsurfer.com

2. Enter "Air Force" into search box.

3. Click the "Surf" button and you will see a list of related web sites.

With factsurfer.com, finding more information is just a click away.

INDEX

★ ★ ★